BigTime® Piano

Kids' Songs

Level 4

Intermediate

This book belongs to: _____

Arranged by

Nancy and Randall Faber

Production Coordinator: Jon Ophoff
Design and Illustration: Terpstra Design, San Francisco
Engraving: Dovetree Productions, Inc.

FABER
PIANO ADVENTURES®

3042 Creek Drive
Ann Arbor, Michigan 48108

A NOTE TO TEACHERS

BigTime® Piano Kids' Songs is a collection of popular songs that bring special enjoyment to students. The sense of fantasy and humor of the selections will motivate and entertain, arranged to give the student a "big" sound while remaining accessible at the intermediate level.

BigTime® Piano Kids' Songs is part of the *BigTime® Piano* series arranged by Faber and Faber. "BigTime" designates Level 4 of the *PreTime® to BigTime® Supplementary Library*. The *BigTime® Piano* series is arranged for the intermediate pianist and it marks a significant achievement for the piano student. As the name implies, "BigTime" selections and arrangements are designed to be fun, showy, and to inspire enthusiasm and pride in the piano student.

Following are the levels of the supplementary library, which lead from *PreTime®* to *BigTime®*.

PreTime® Piano	(Primer Level)
PlayTime® Piano	(Level 1)
ShowTime® Piano	(Level 2A)
ChordTime® Piano	(Level 2B)
FunTime® Piano	(Level 3A – 3B)
BigTime® Piano	(Level 4)

Each level offers books in a variety of styles, making it possible for the teacher to offer stimulating material for every student. For a complimentary detailed listing, e-mail faber@pianoadventures.com or write us at the address below.

Visit **www.PianoAdventures.com**.

Helpful Hints:

1. Music is social, too. Students who memorize a couple of songs from this book are always ready to share at parties and for friends.

2. As rhythm is of prime importance, encourage the student to feel the rhythm in his/her body when playing music. This can be accomplished with the tapping of the toe or heel, and with clapping exercises.

3. The songs can be assigned in any order. Selection is usually best made by the student, according to interest and enthusiasm.

4. Chord symbols are given above the treble staff. Time taken to help the student see how chords are used in the arrangement is time well spent. Such work can help memory, sight-reading, and even help the student build improvisation, composition and arranging skills.

ISBN 978-1-61677-629-9

TABLE OF CONTENTS

Linus and Lucy

By VINCE GUARALDI

6

(Meet) The Flintstones

Words and Music by
WILLIAM HANNA, JOSEPH BARBERA
and HOYT S. CURTIN

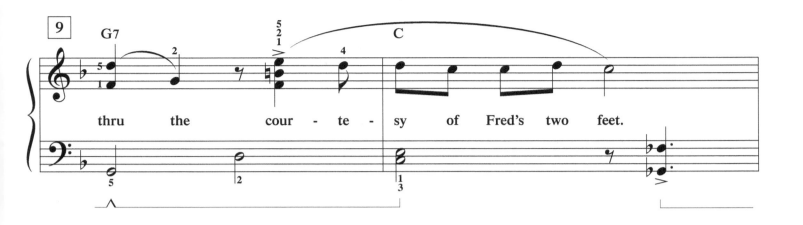

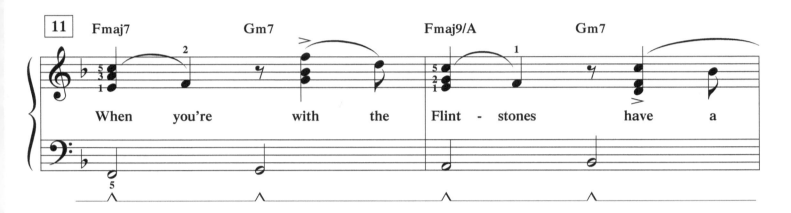

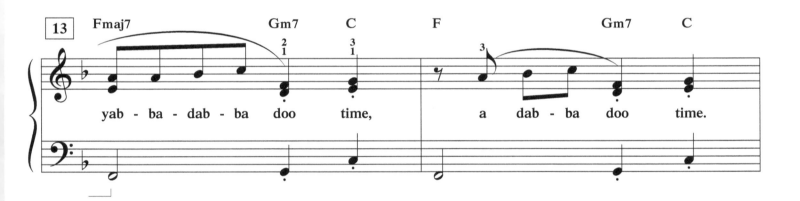

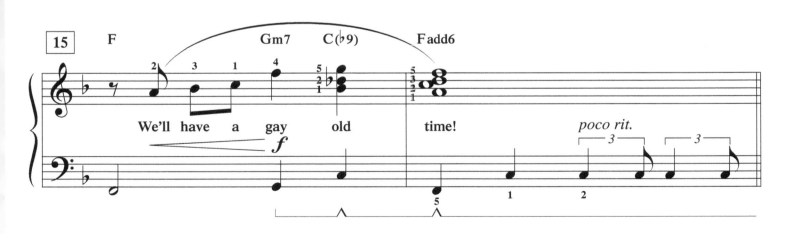

8

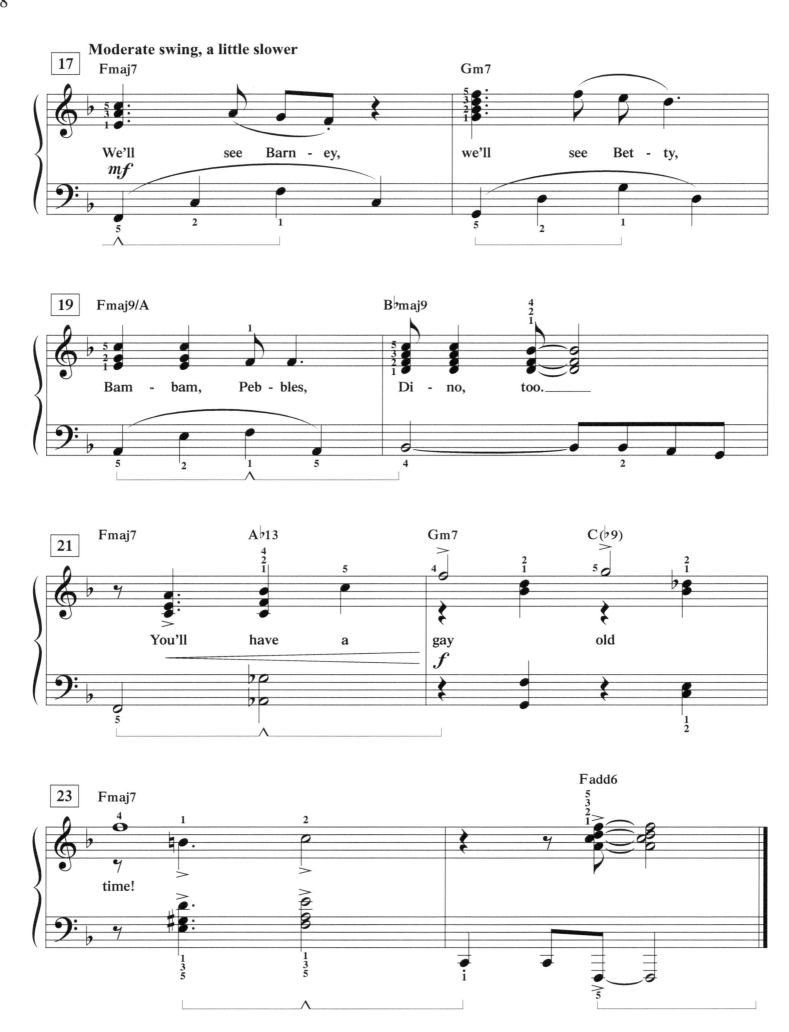

Cruella De Vil

from Walt Disney's *101 Dalmatians*

Words and Music by
MEL LEVEN

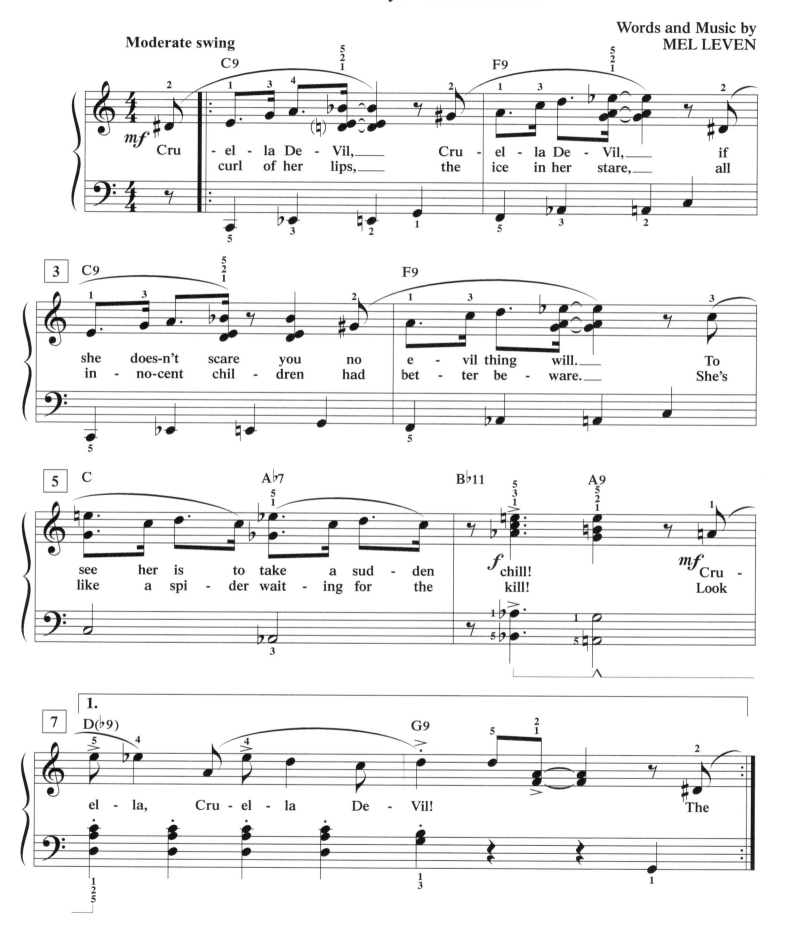

FF3005

10

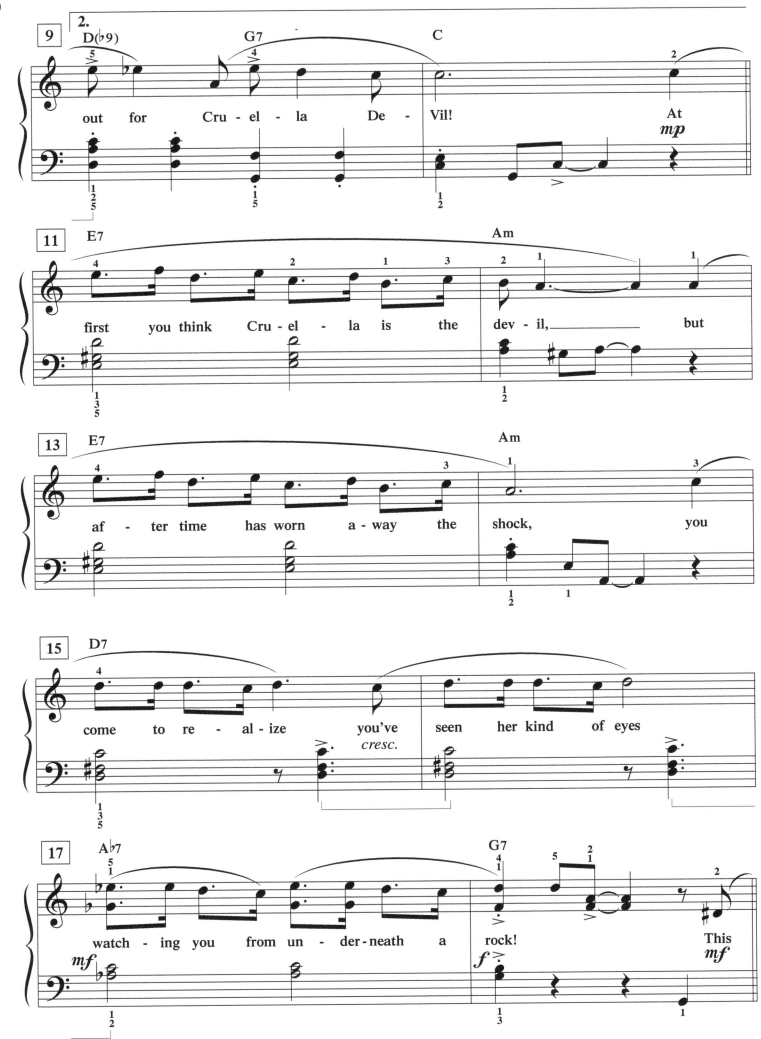

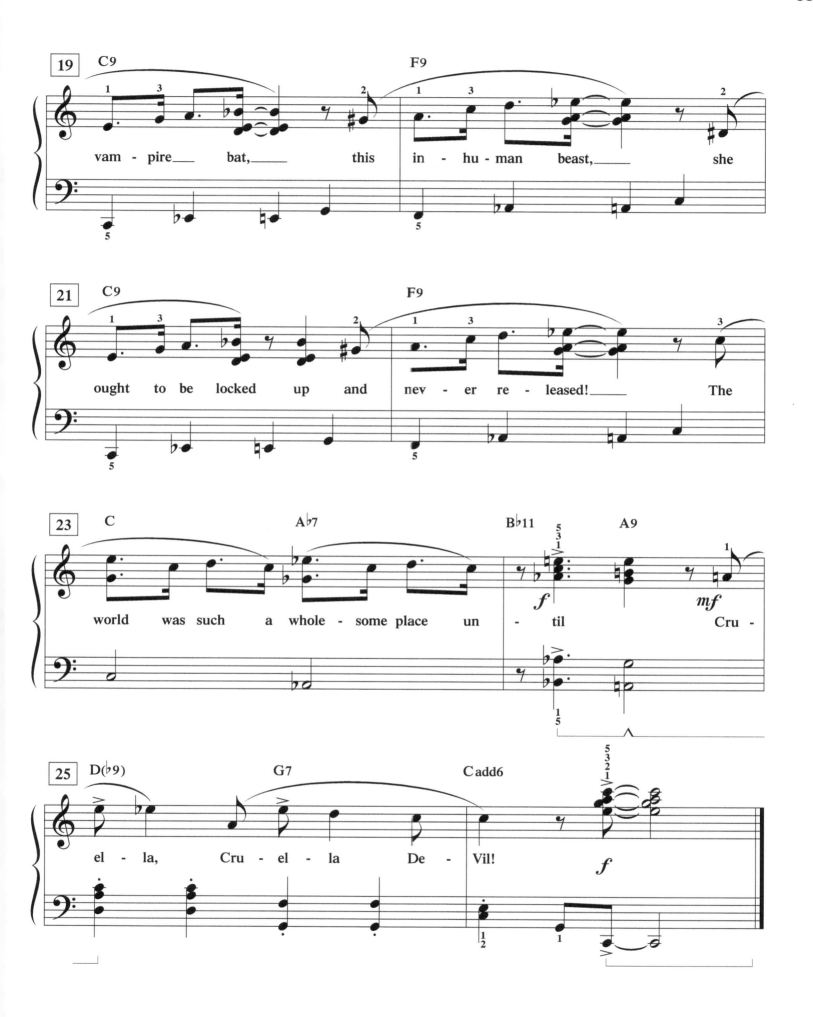

Thank You for Being a Friend

Words and Music by
ANDREW GOLD

14

you would see___ the big-gest gift would be from me,   and the

card   at - tached would say,___ Thank you for be - in' a friend.

Thank you for be - in' a friend.___   Thank you for be - in' a friend.

Thank you for   be - in'   a friend.___

molto rit.

sfz

Once Upon a Dream

from Walt Disney's *Sleeping Beauty*

Words and Music by
SAMMY FAIN and JACK LAWRENCE
Adapted from a Theme by Tchaikovsky

FF3005

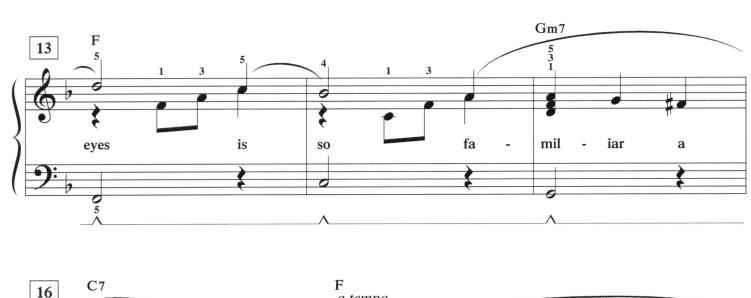

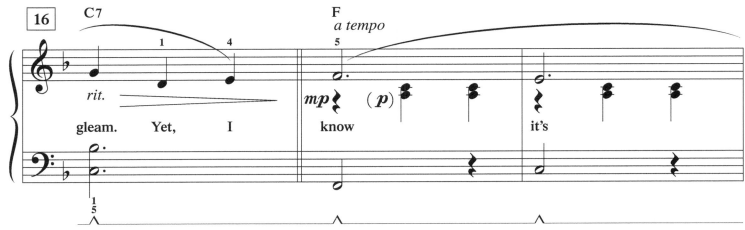

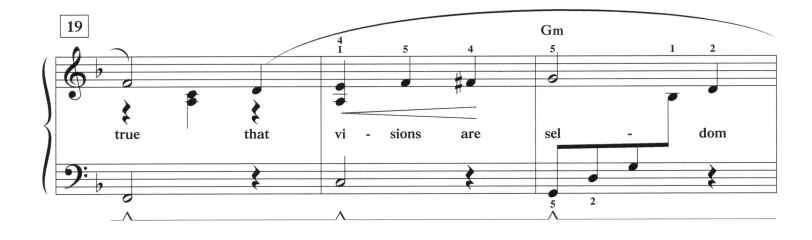

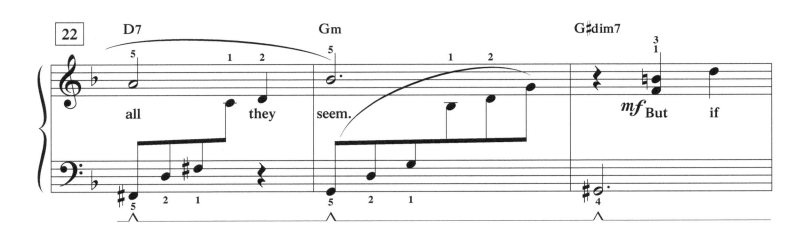

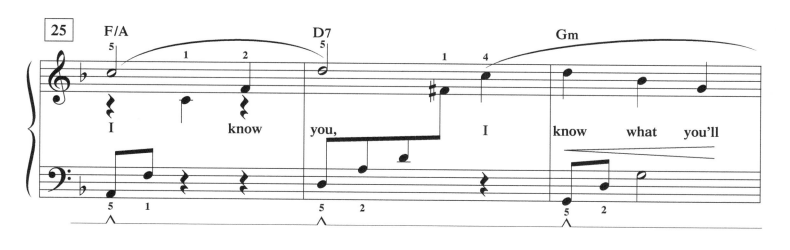

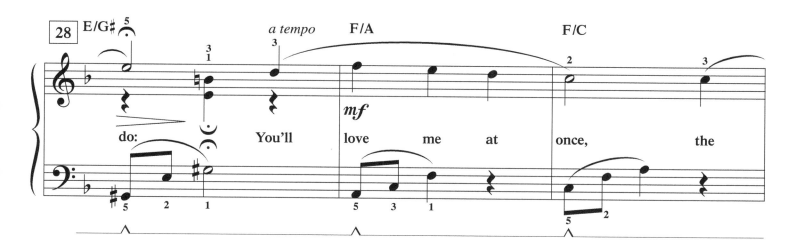

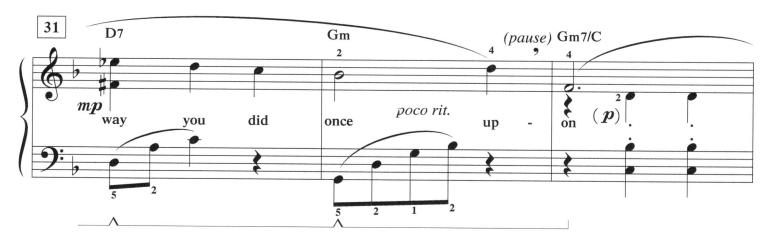

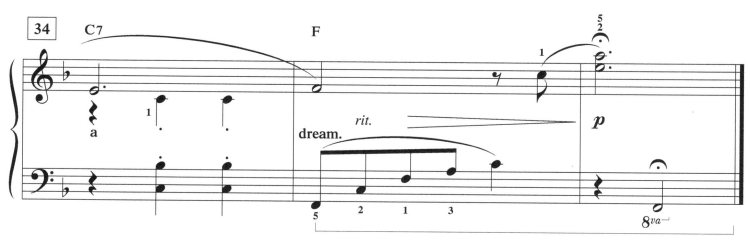

The Pink Panther

from THE PINK PANTHER

Music by
HENRY MANCINI

20

In Dreams

from the New Line Cinema feature presentation
The Lord of the Rings: The Fellowship of the Ring

Words and Music by
FRAN WALSH and HOWARD SHORE

24

When the seas and moun - tains fall and we come to end of days,_____ in the dark I hear a call, call - ing me there._____ I will go there and back a - gain.

FF3005

My Favorite Things

from *The Sound of Music*

Lyrics by OSCAR HAMMERSTEIN II
Music by RICHARD RODGERS

FF3005

26

Can You Feel the Love Tonight

from Walt Disney's *The Lion King*

Music by ELTON JOHN
Lyrics by TIM RICE

30

Additional Lyrics

There's a time for everyone, if they only learn
That the twisting kaleidoscope moves us all in turn.
There's a rhyme and reason to the wild outdoors
When the heart of this star-crossed voyager beats in time with yours. *To Chorus*

Hakuna Matata

from Walt Disney's THE LION KING

Music by ELTON JOHN
Lyrics by TIM RICE

FF3005

32

Flight of the Bumblebee

NIKOLAI RIMSKY-KORSAKOV

Fast, but steady

I'm a Believer

Words and Music by
NEIL DIAMOND

40